BLACK GIRLS COLOR

Book Design by HMDpublishing

This book belongs to

. . . .

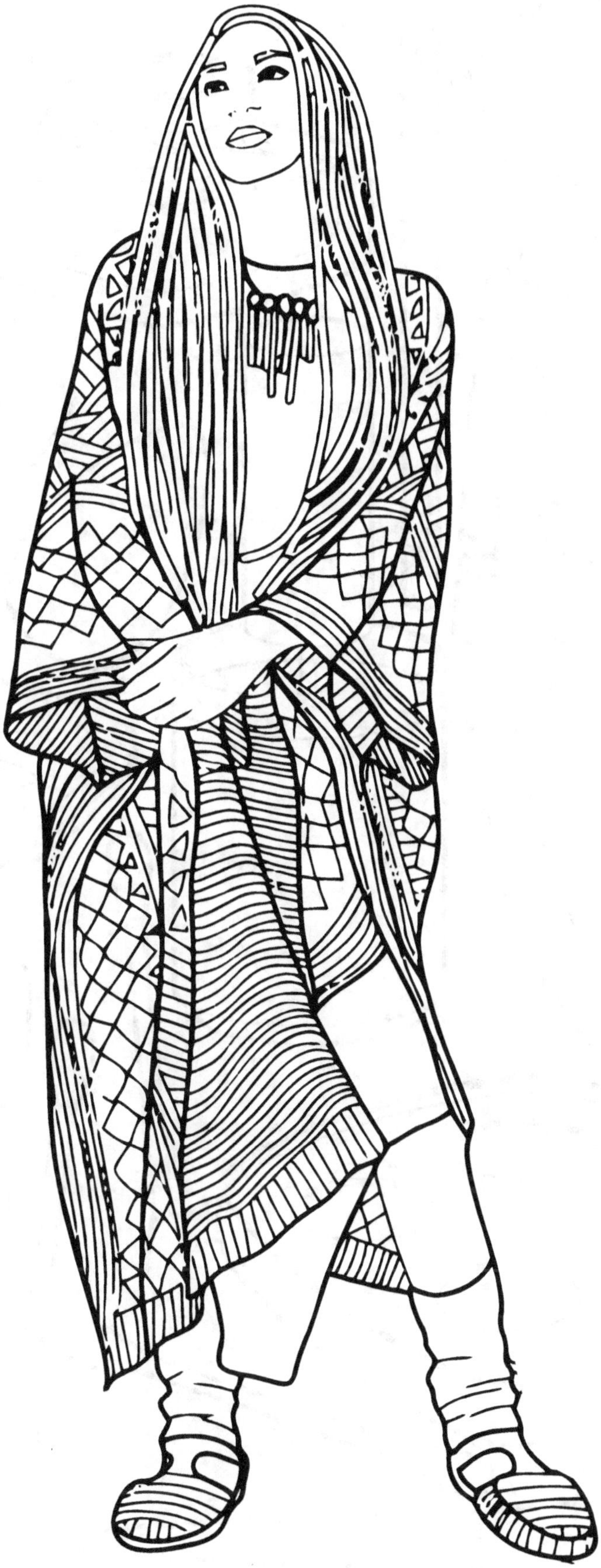

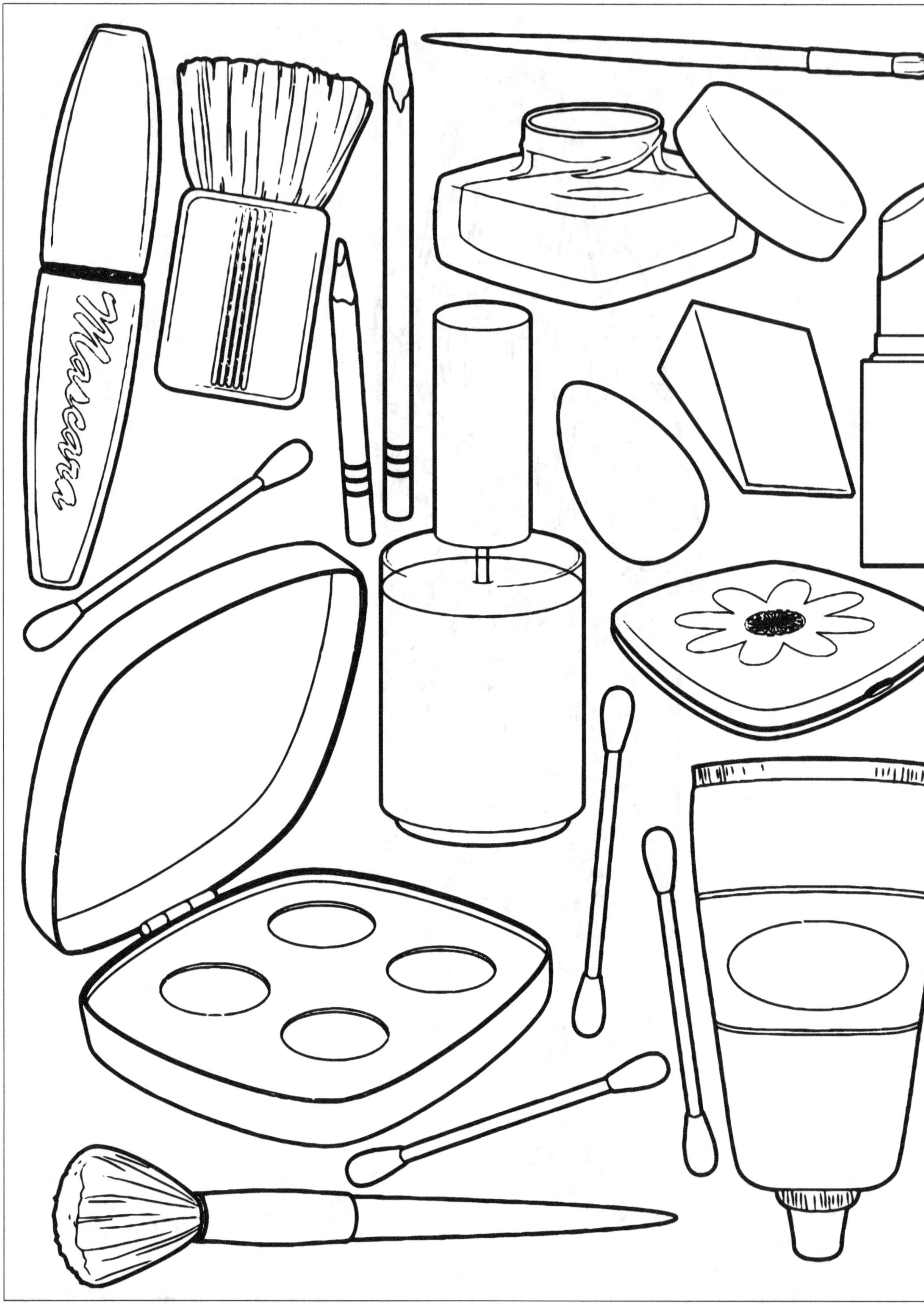
Mascara

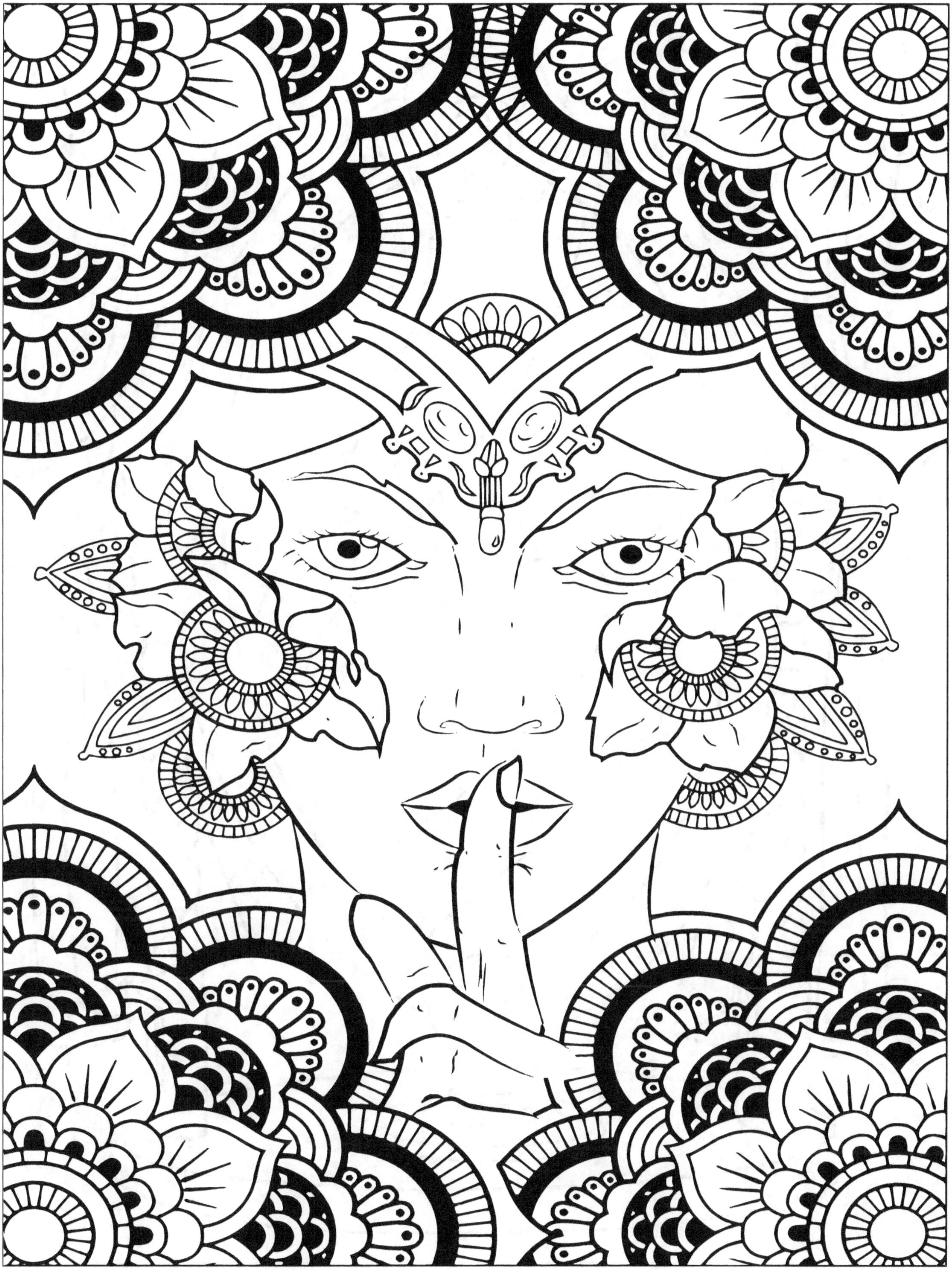

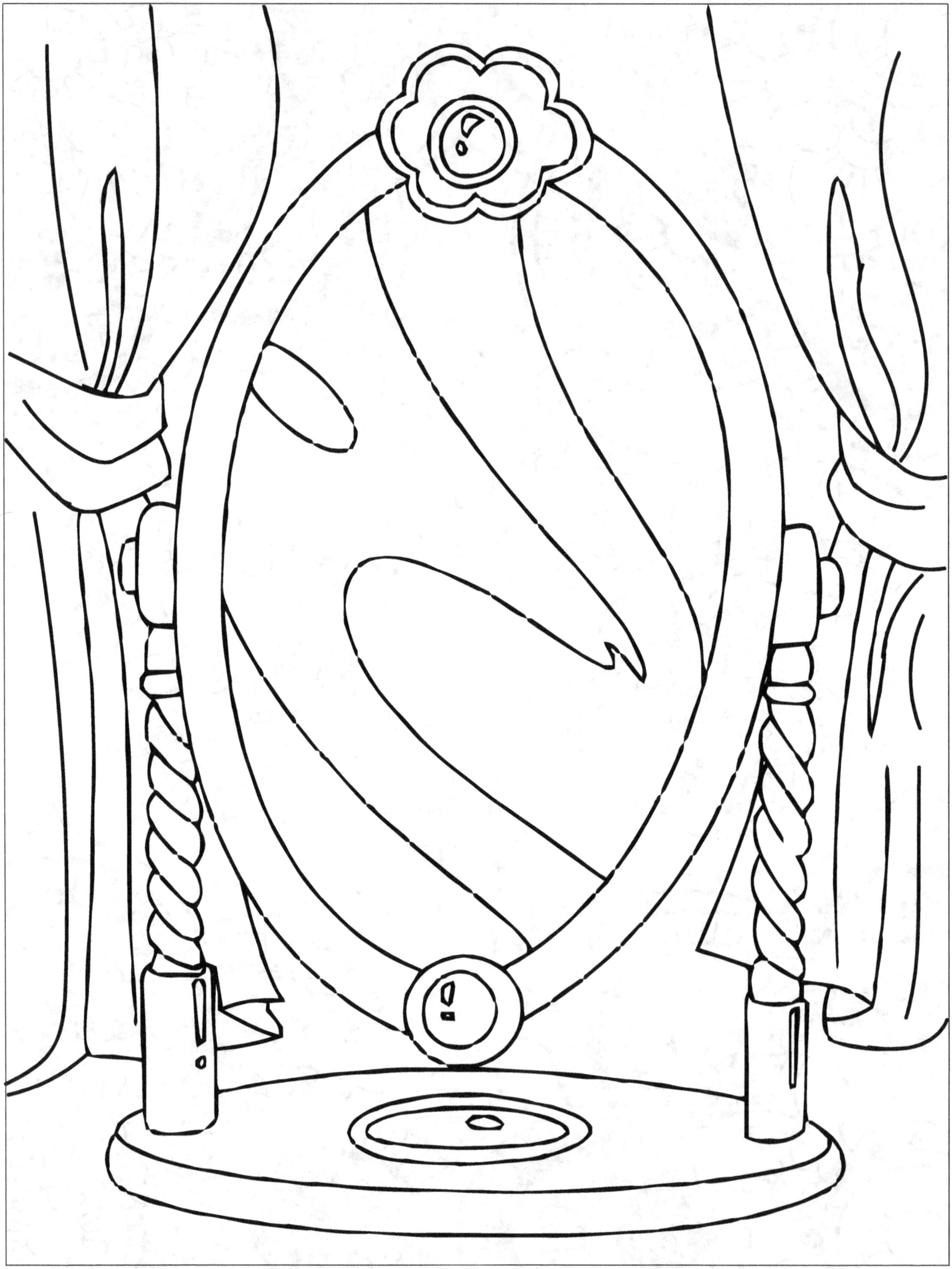

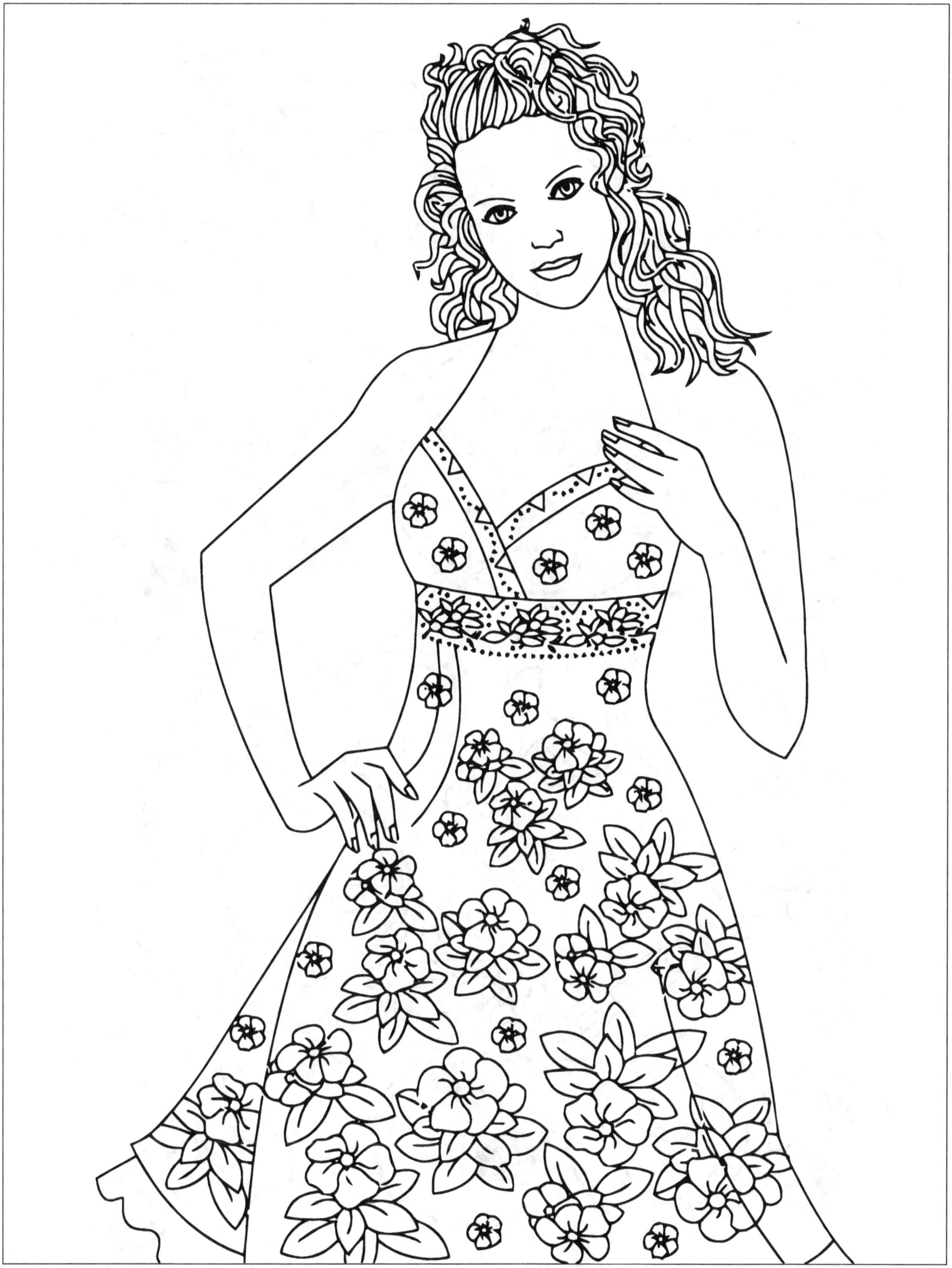

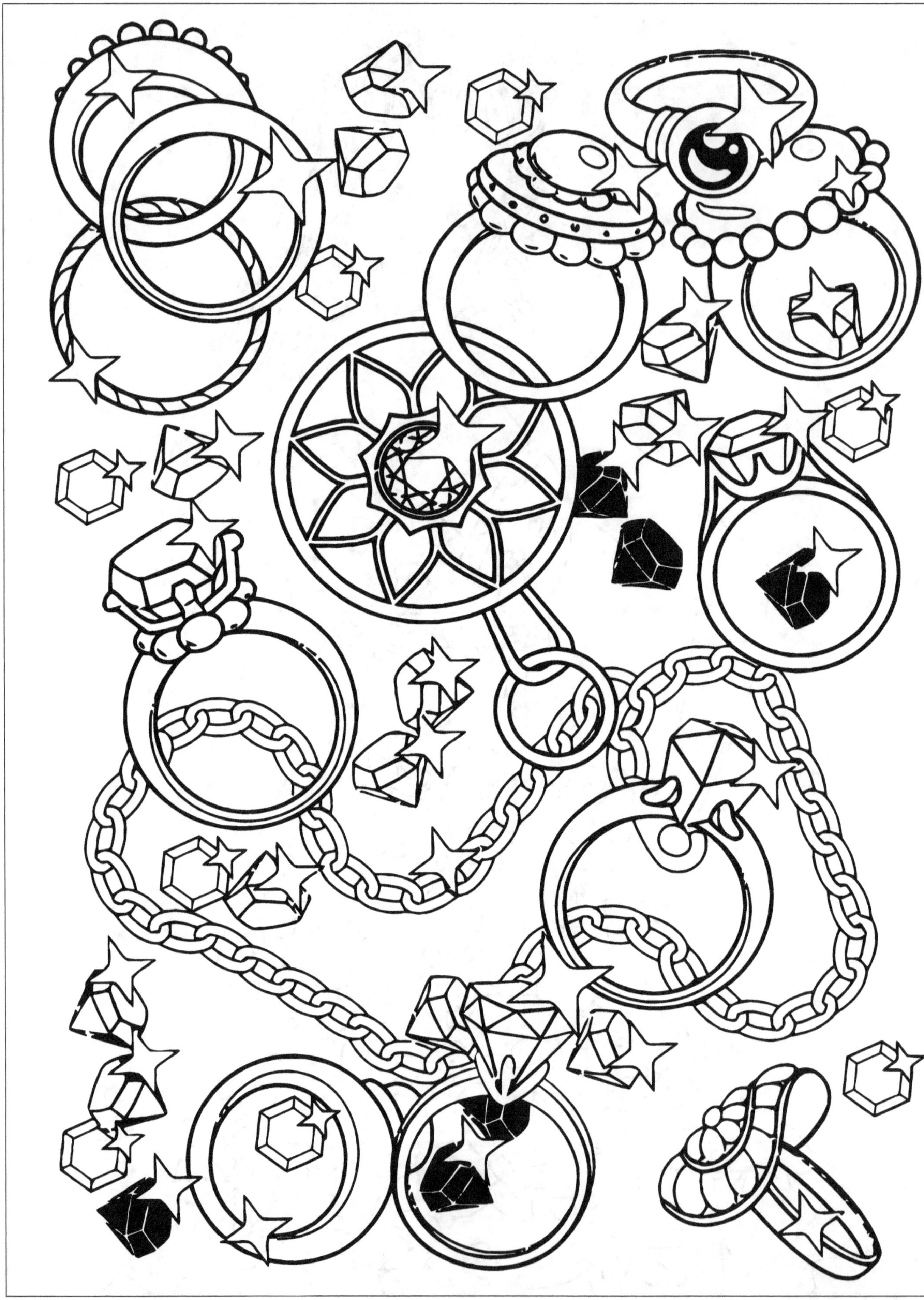

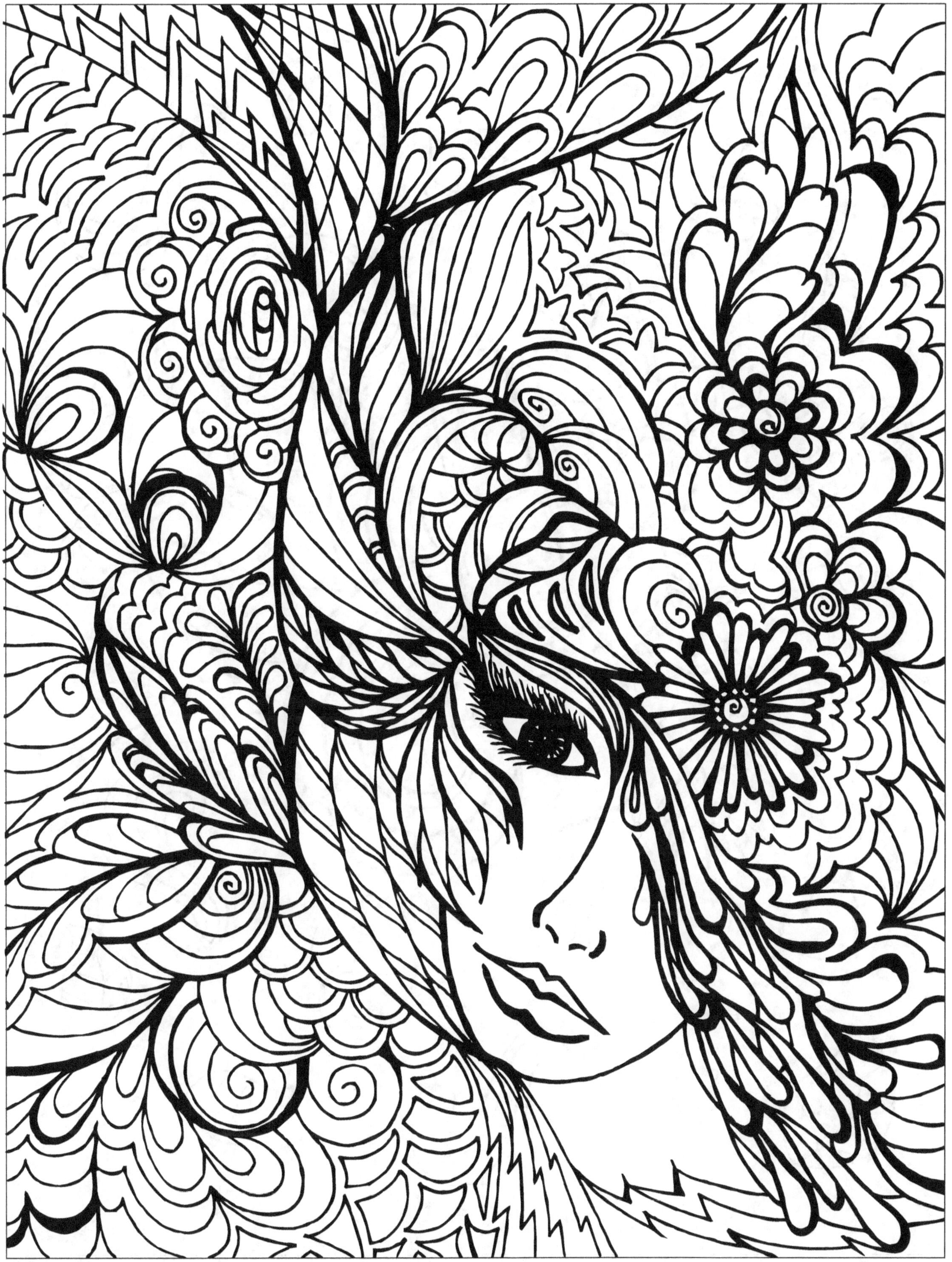

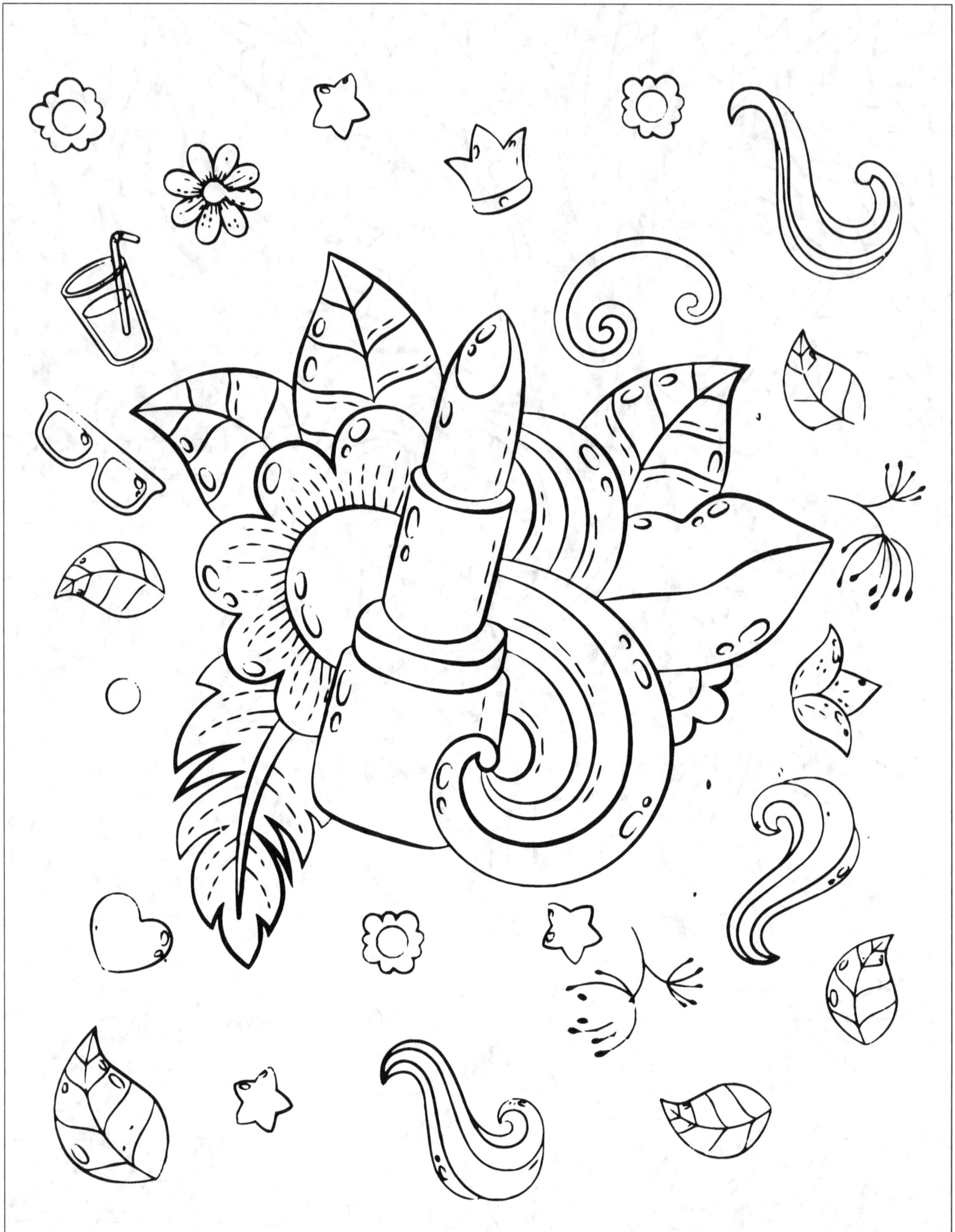

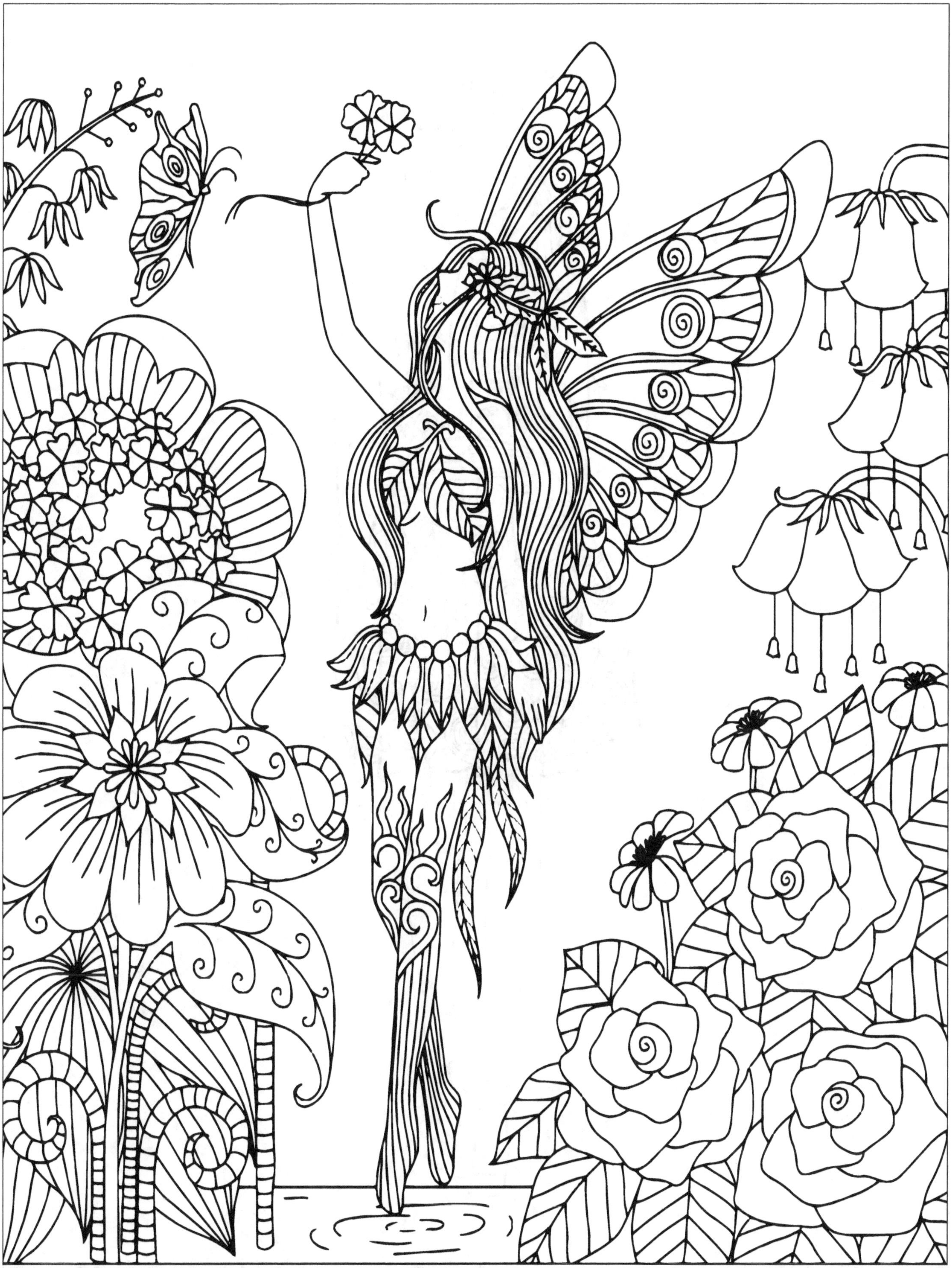

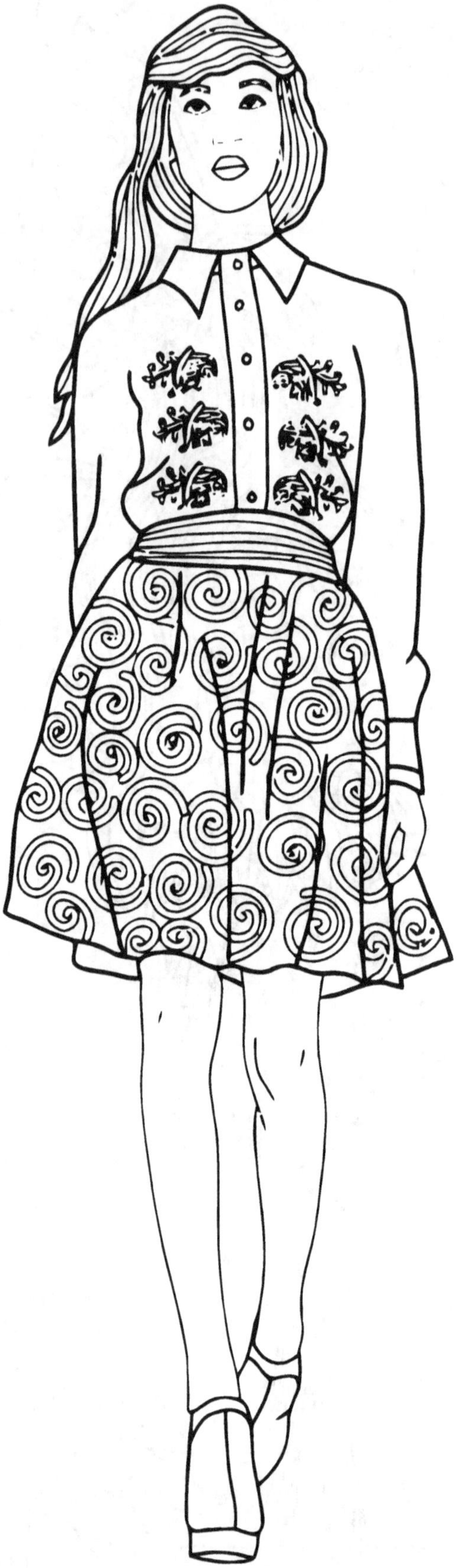

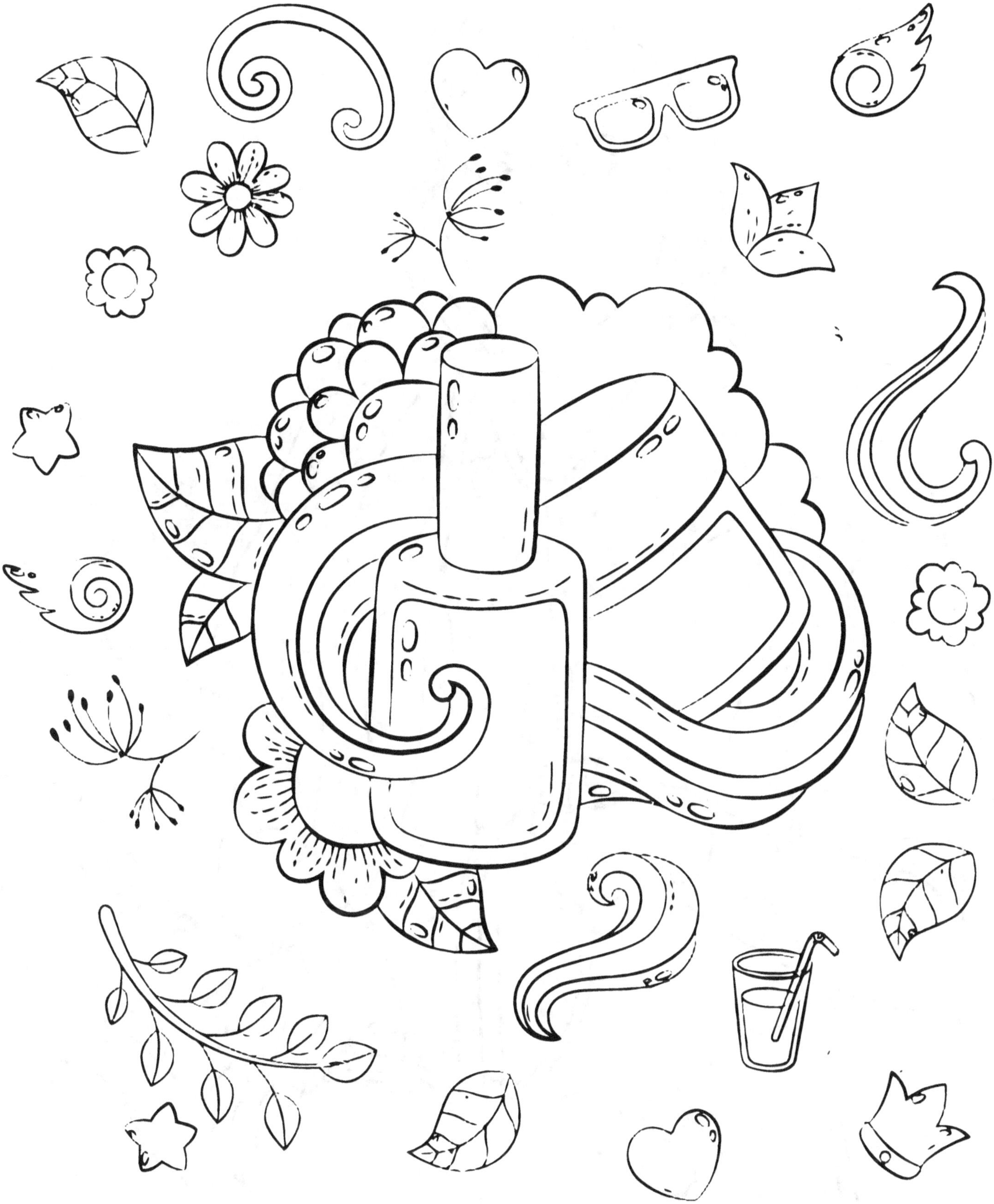

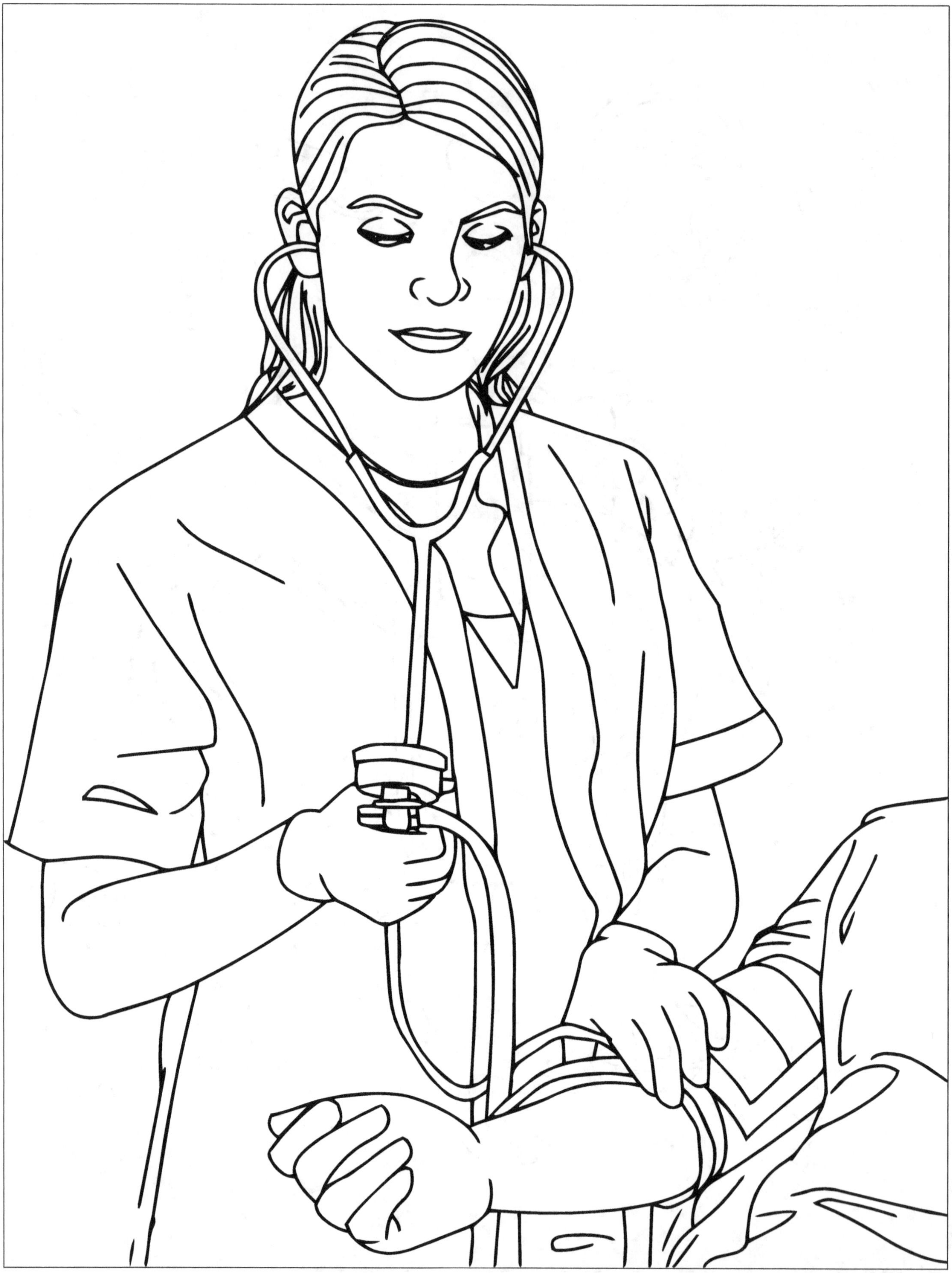

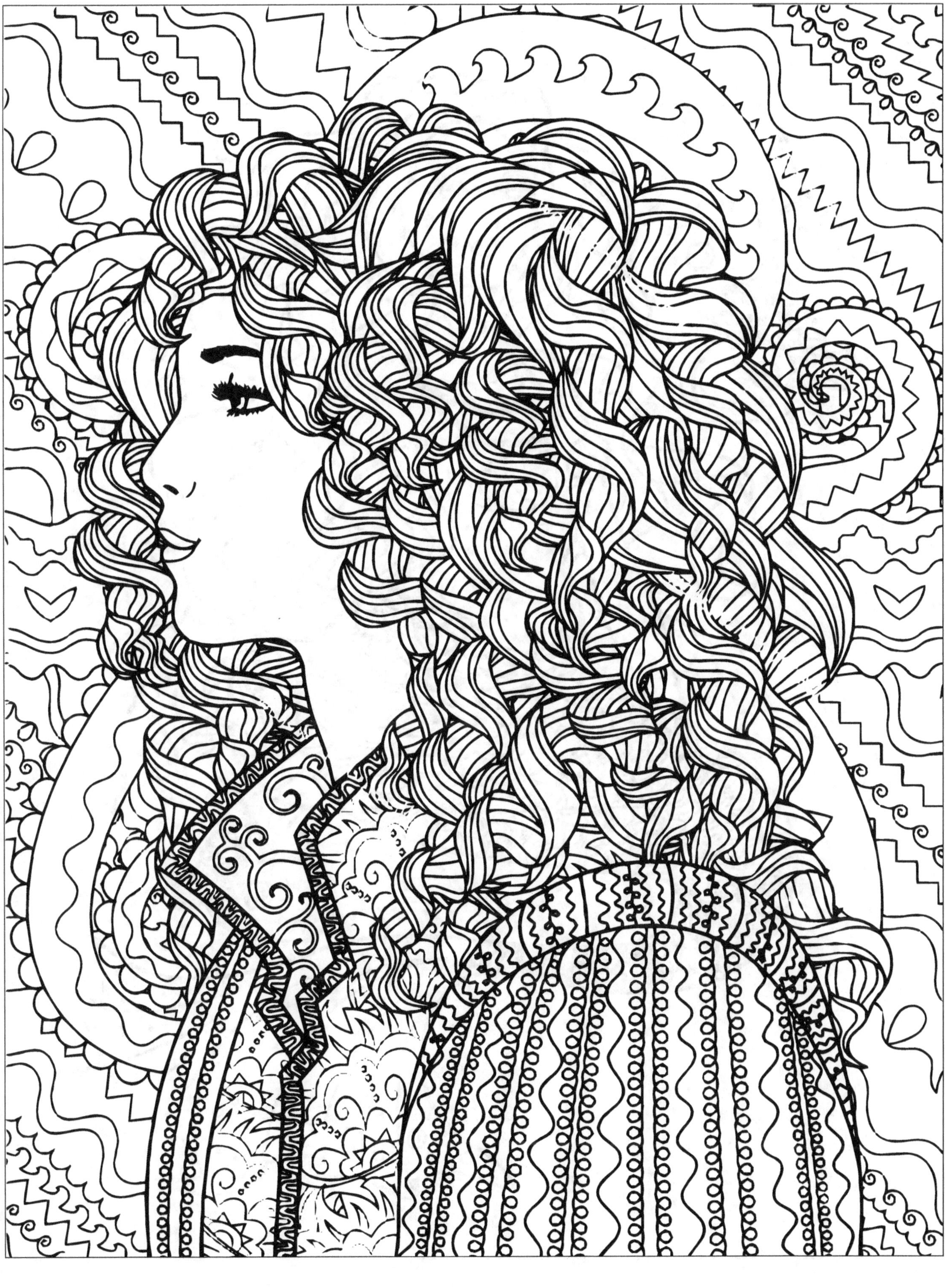

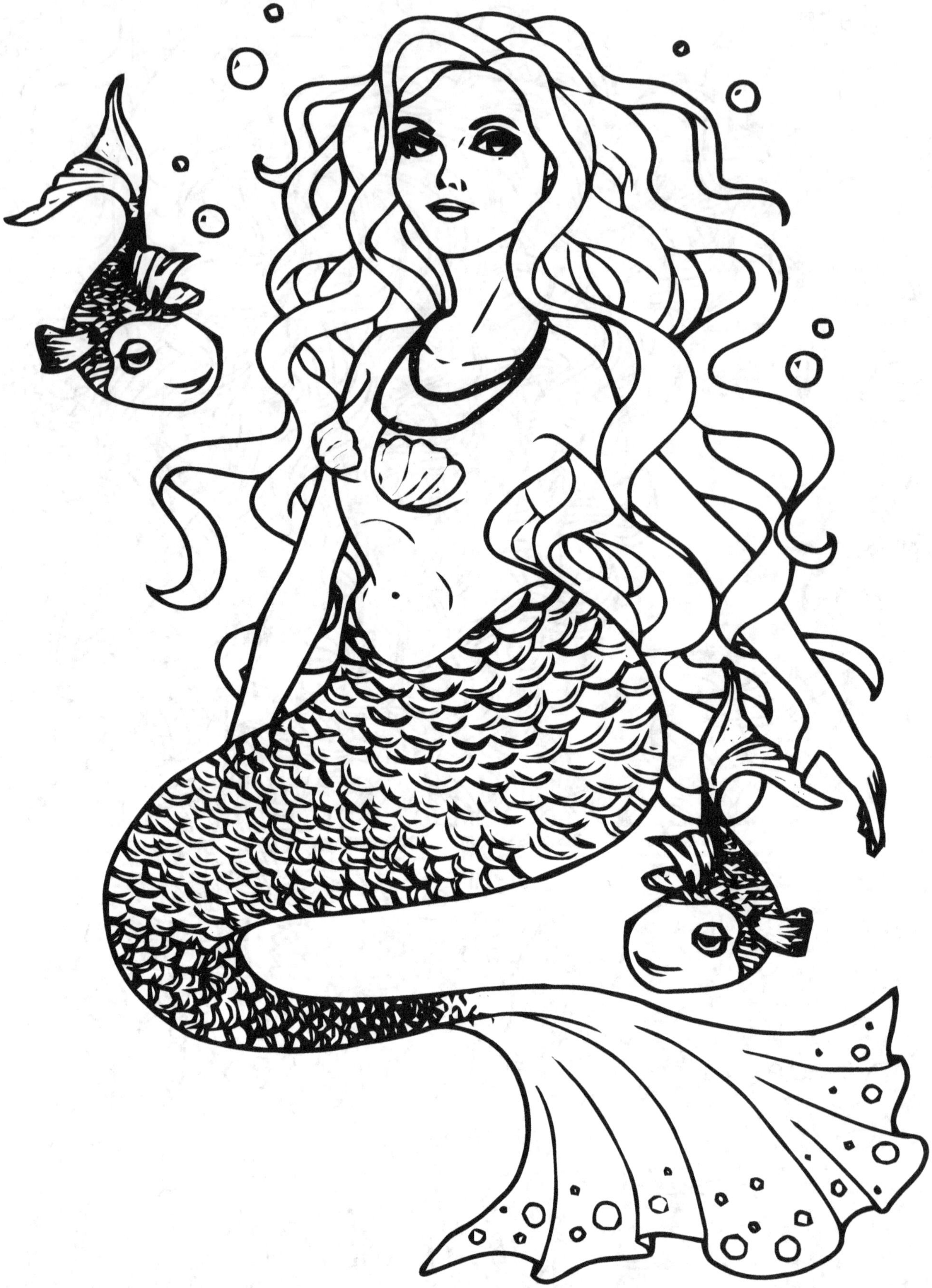

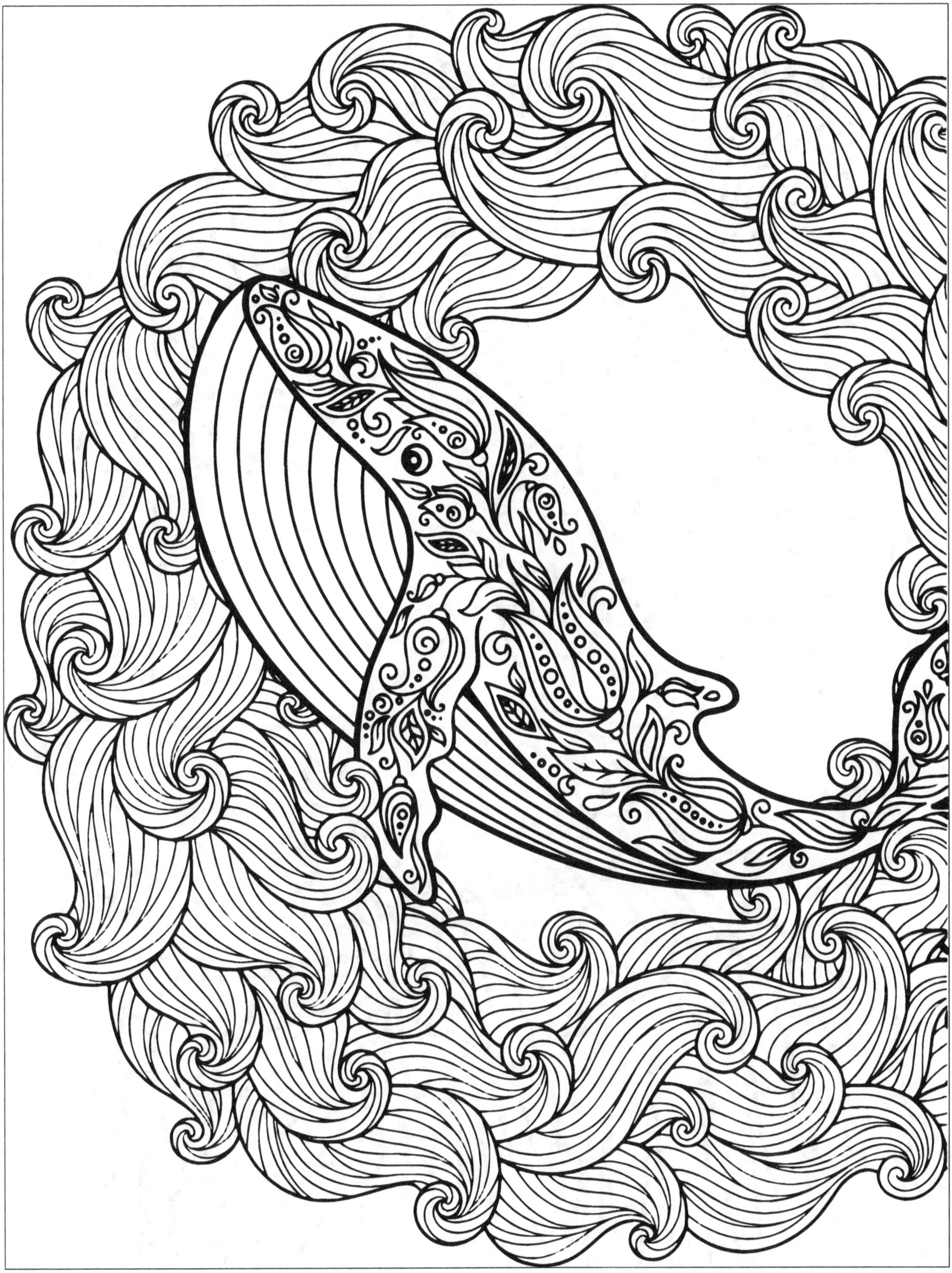

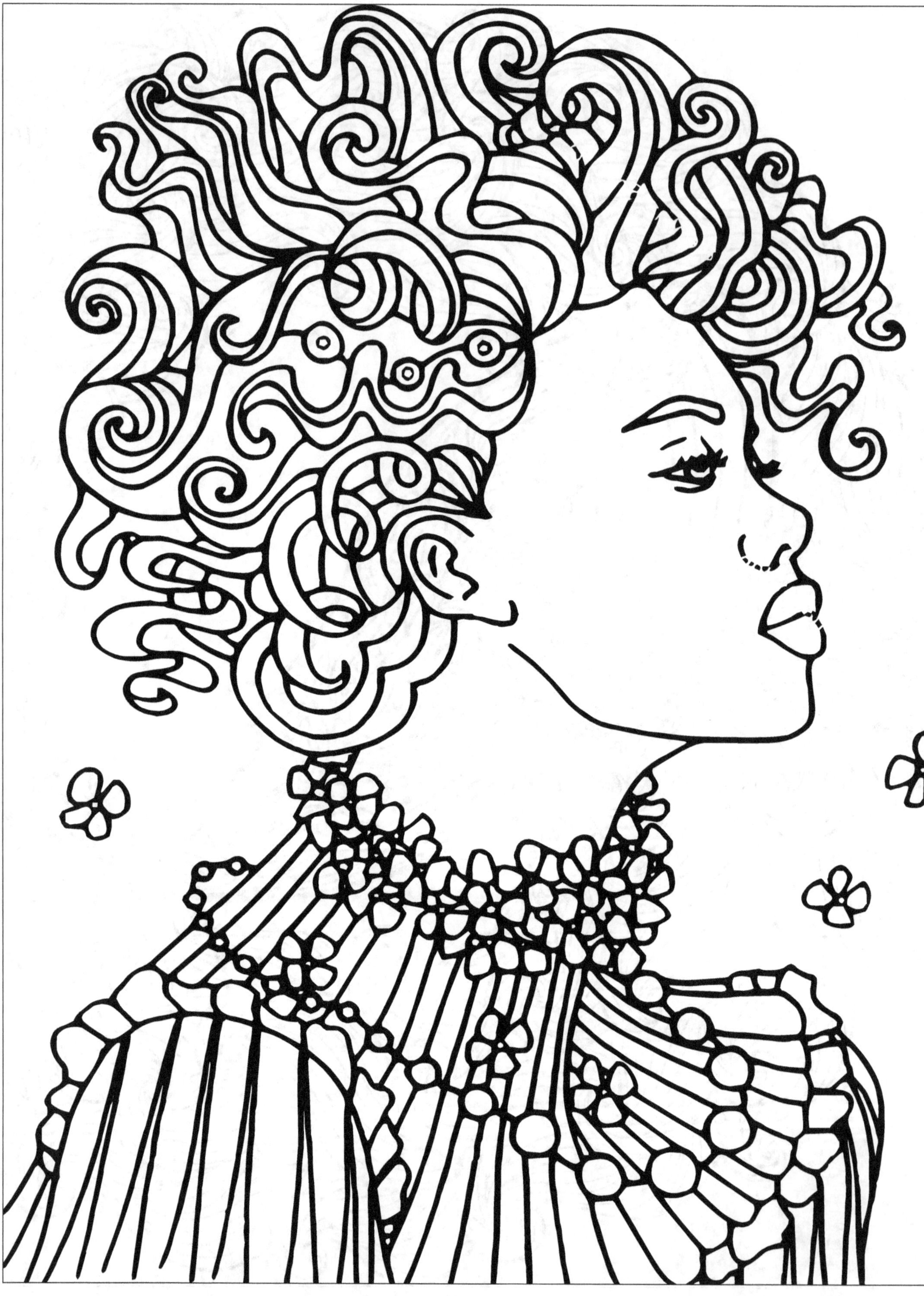

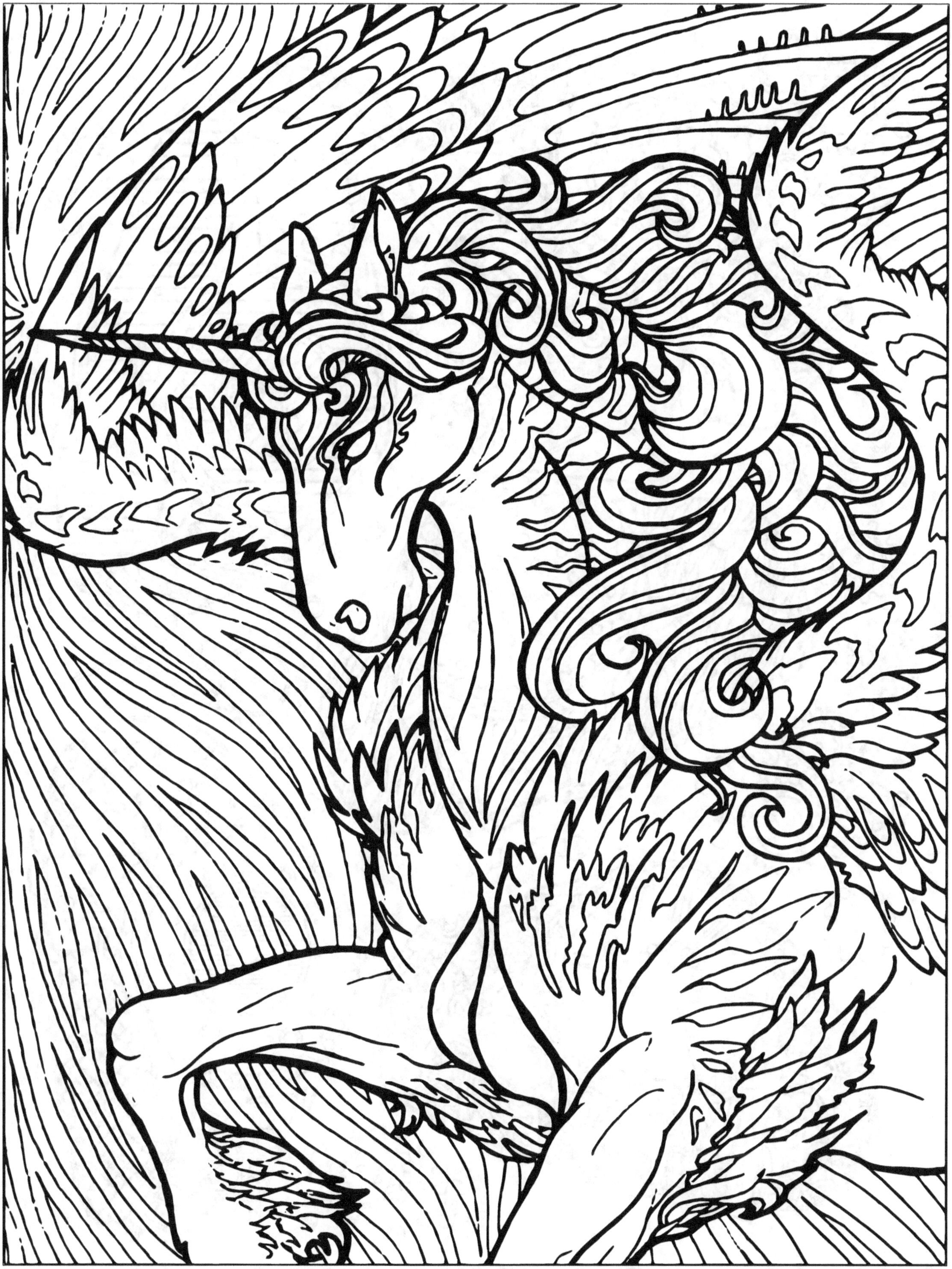

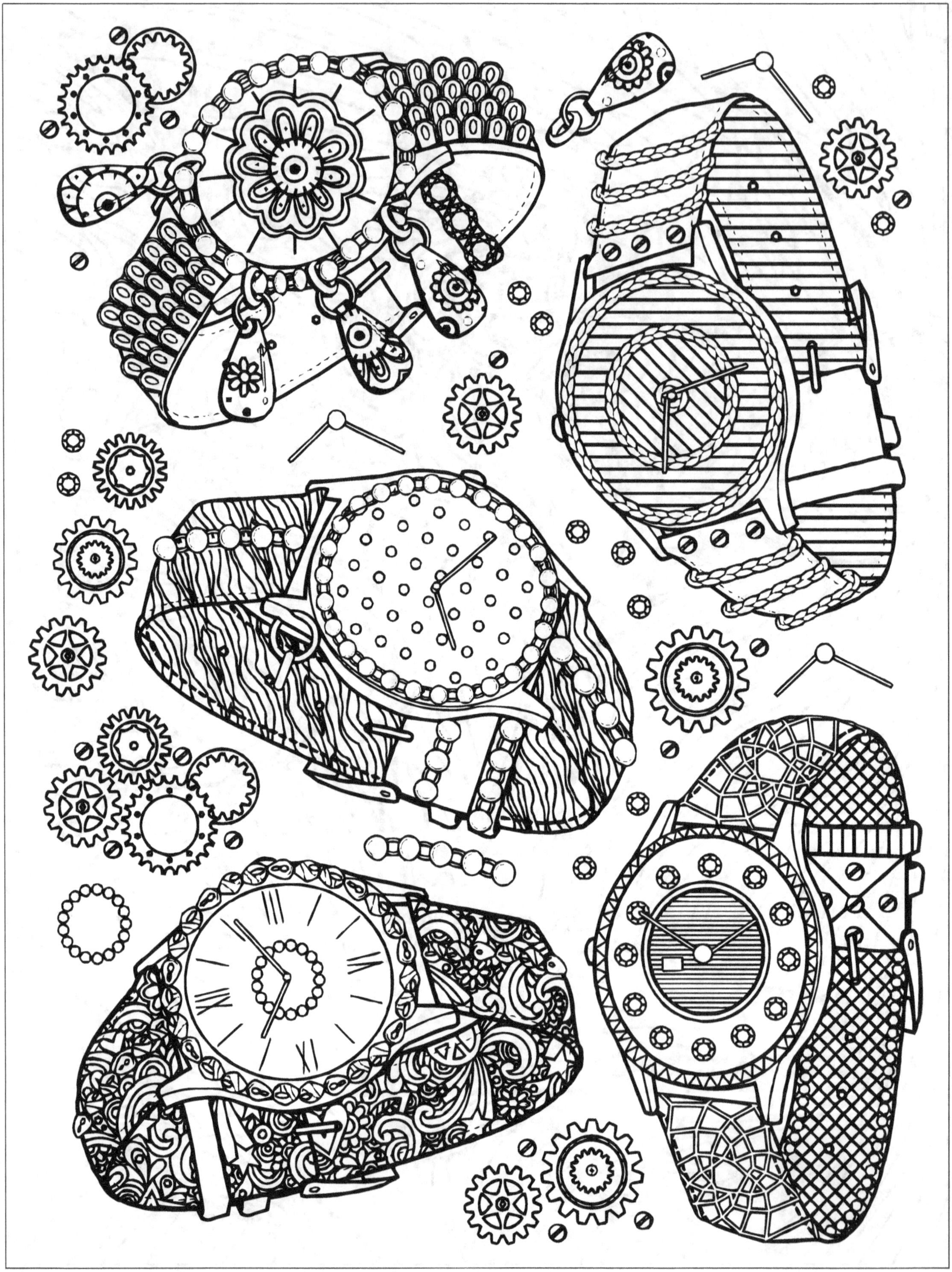

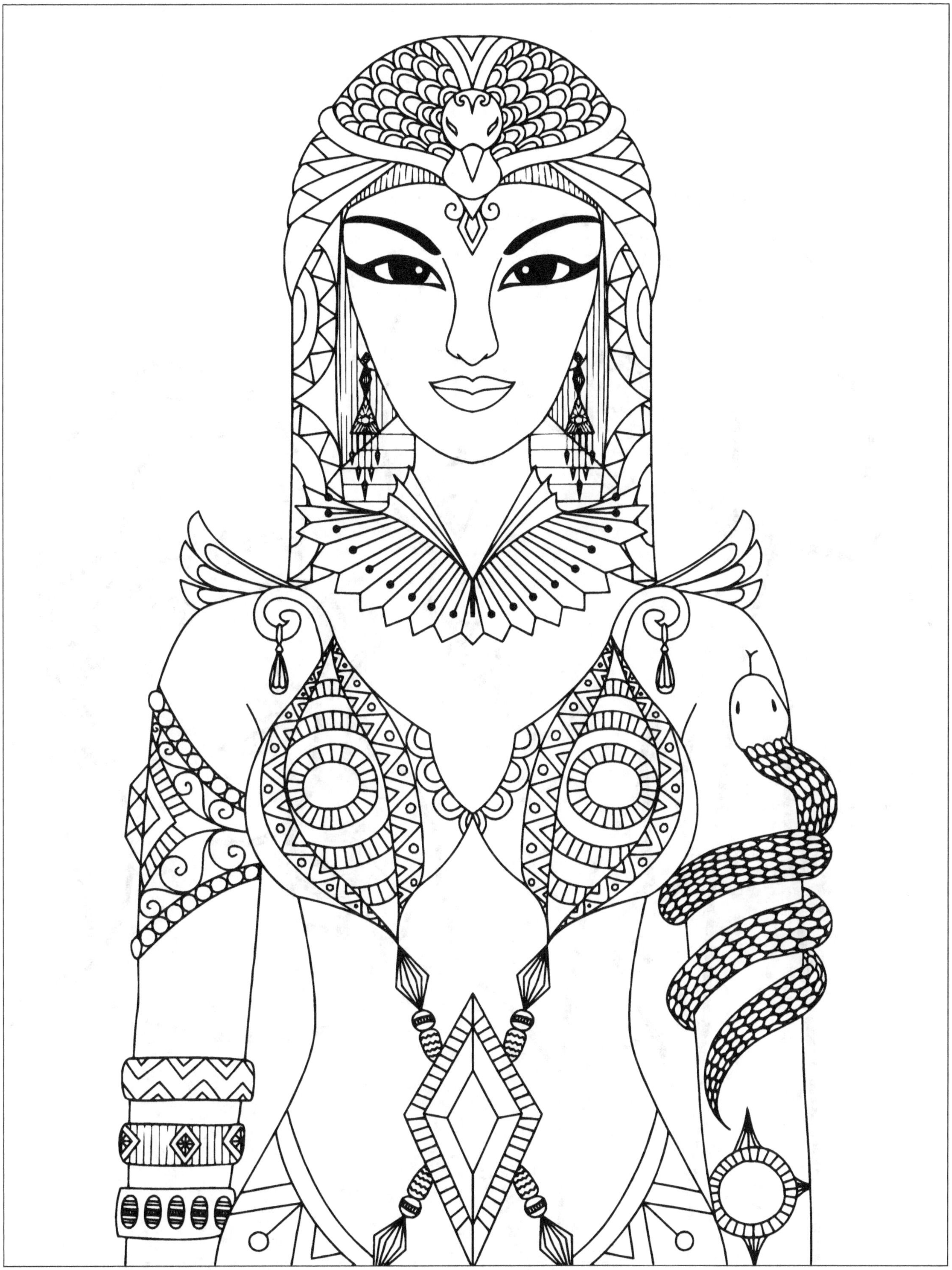

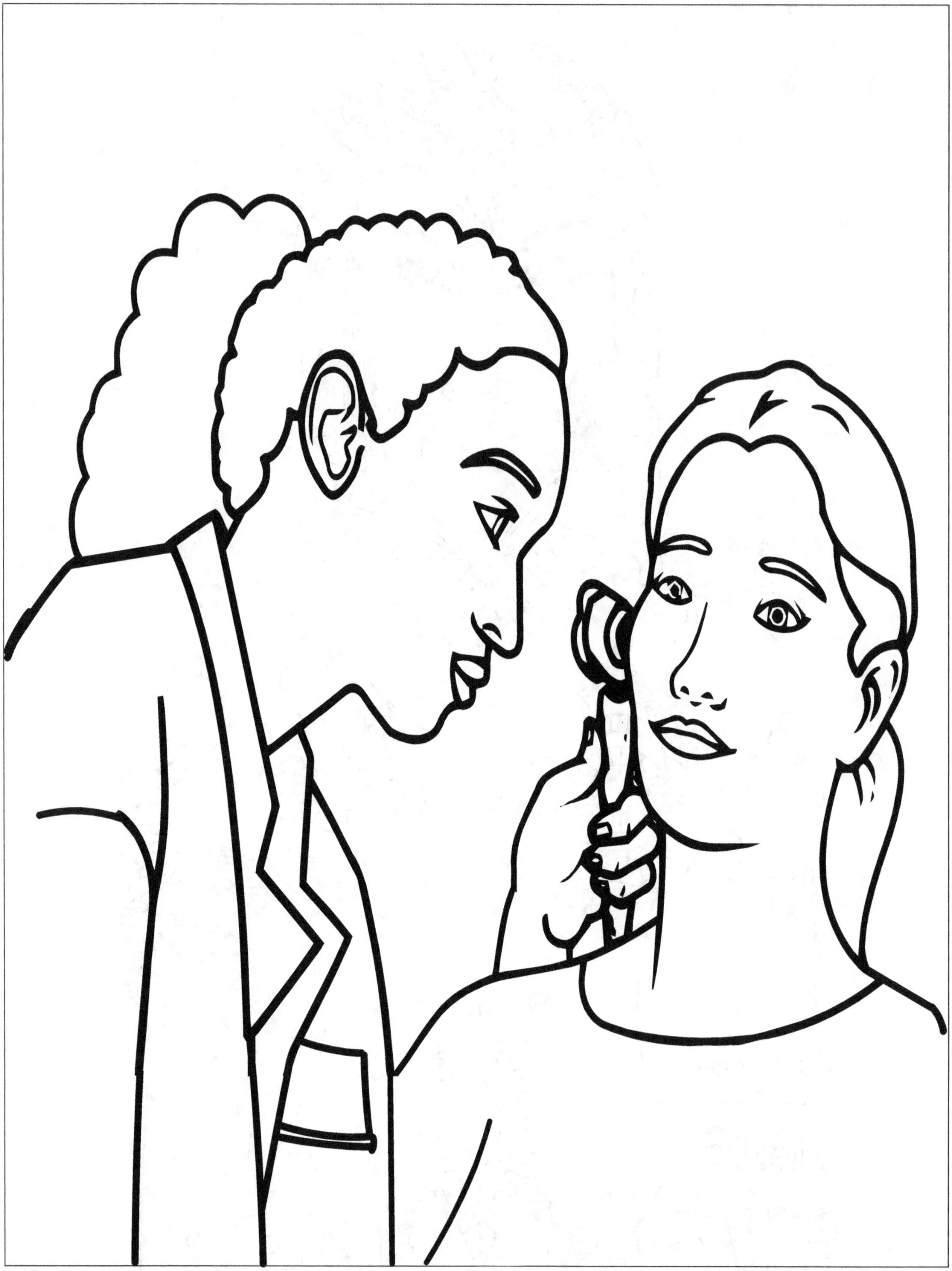

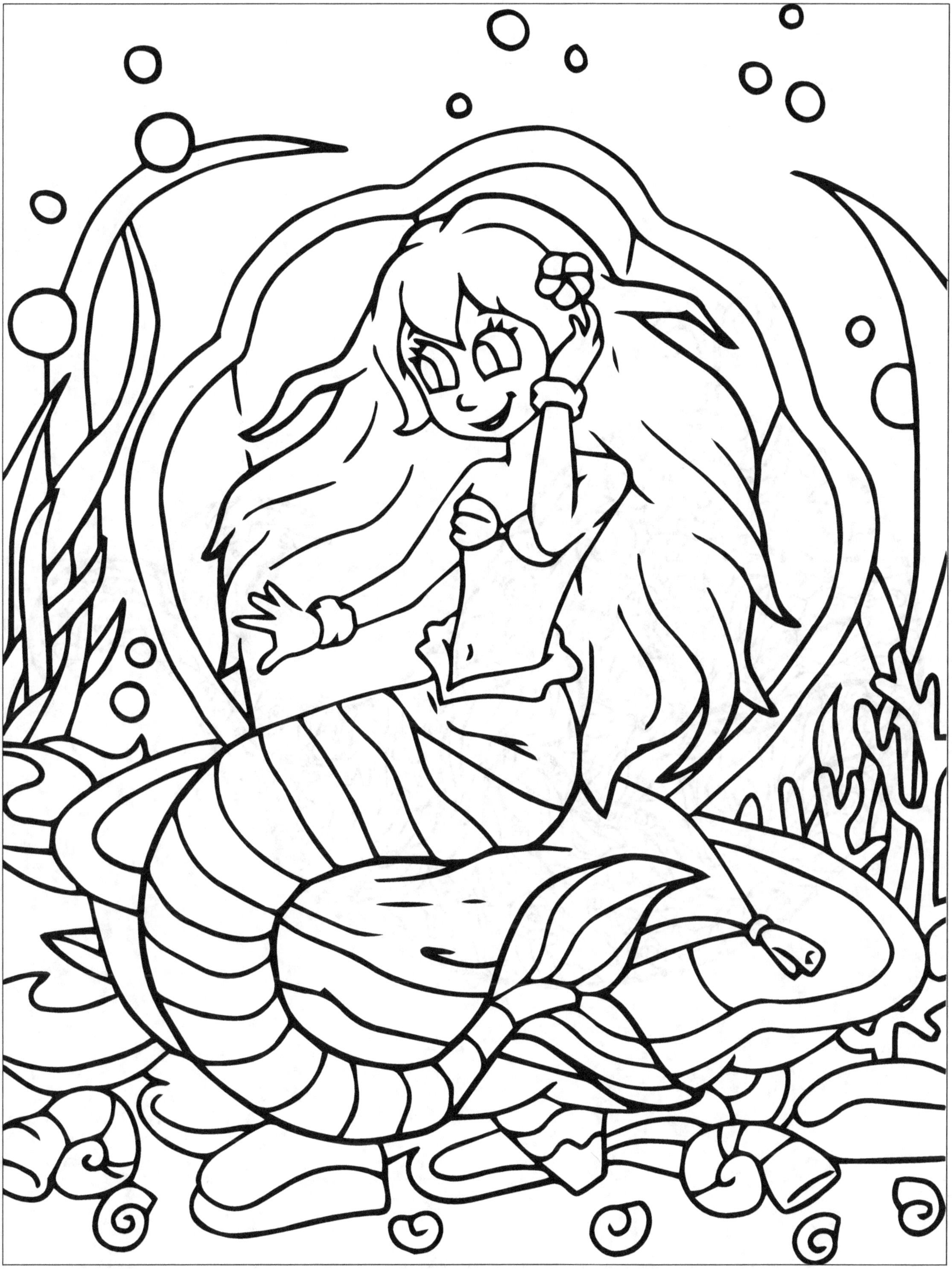

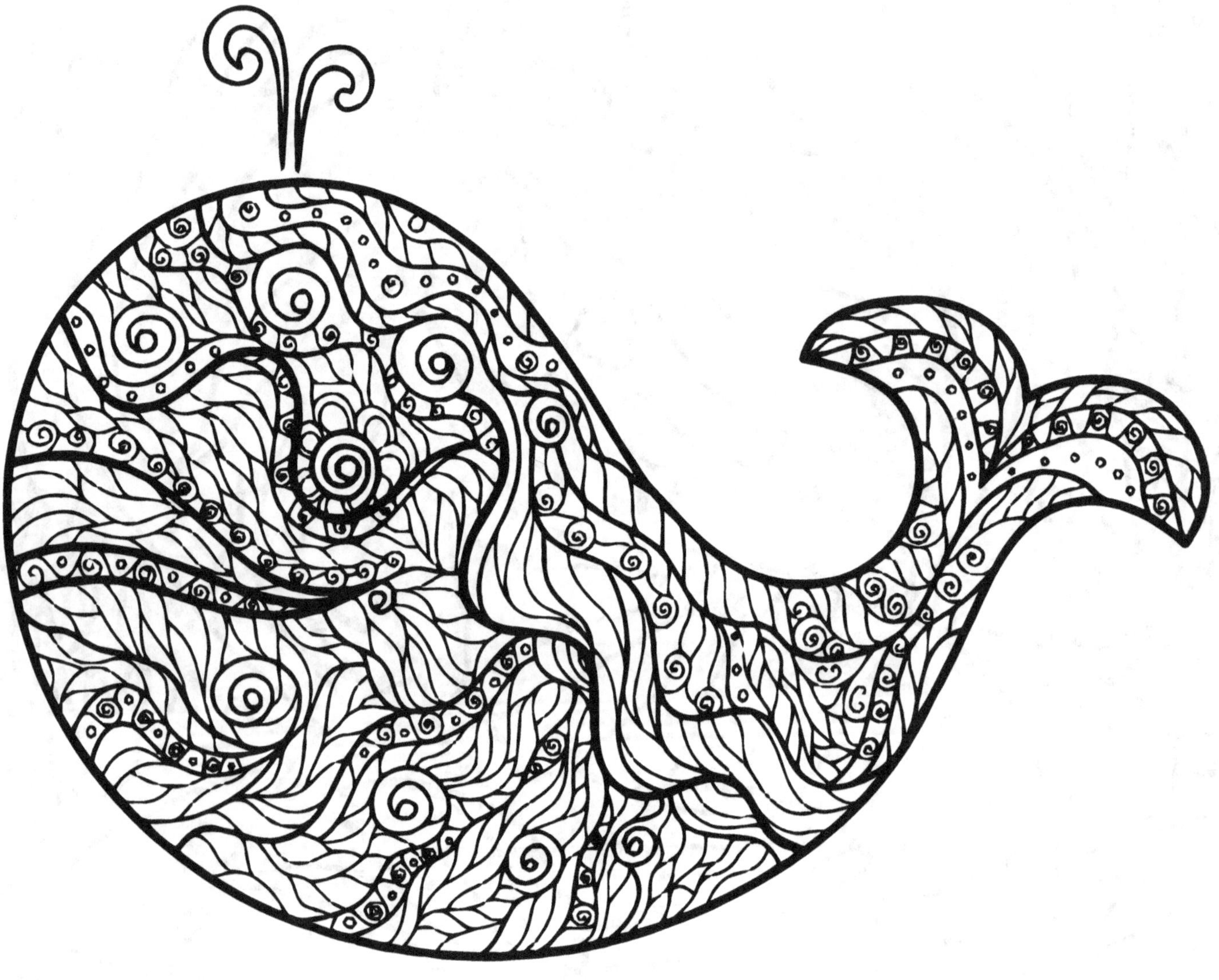

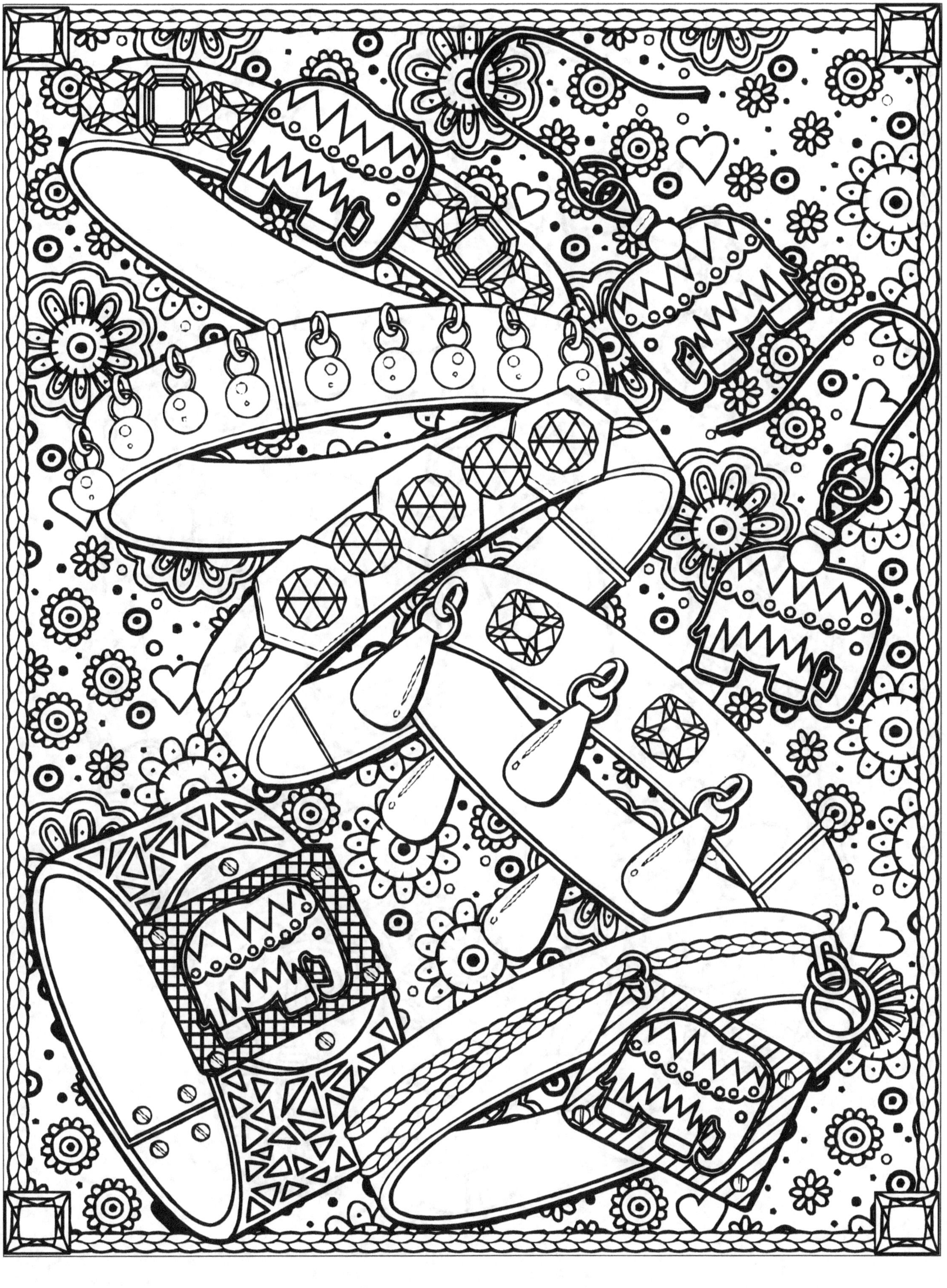

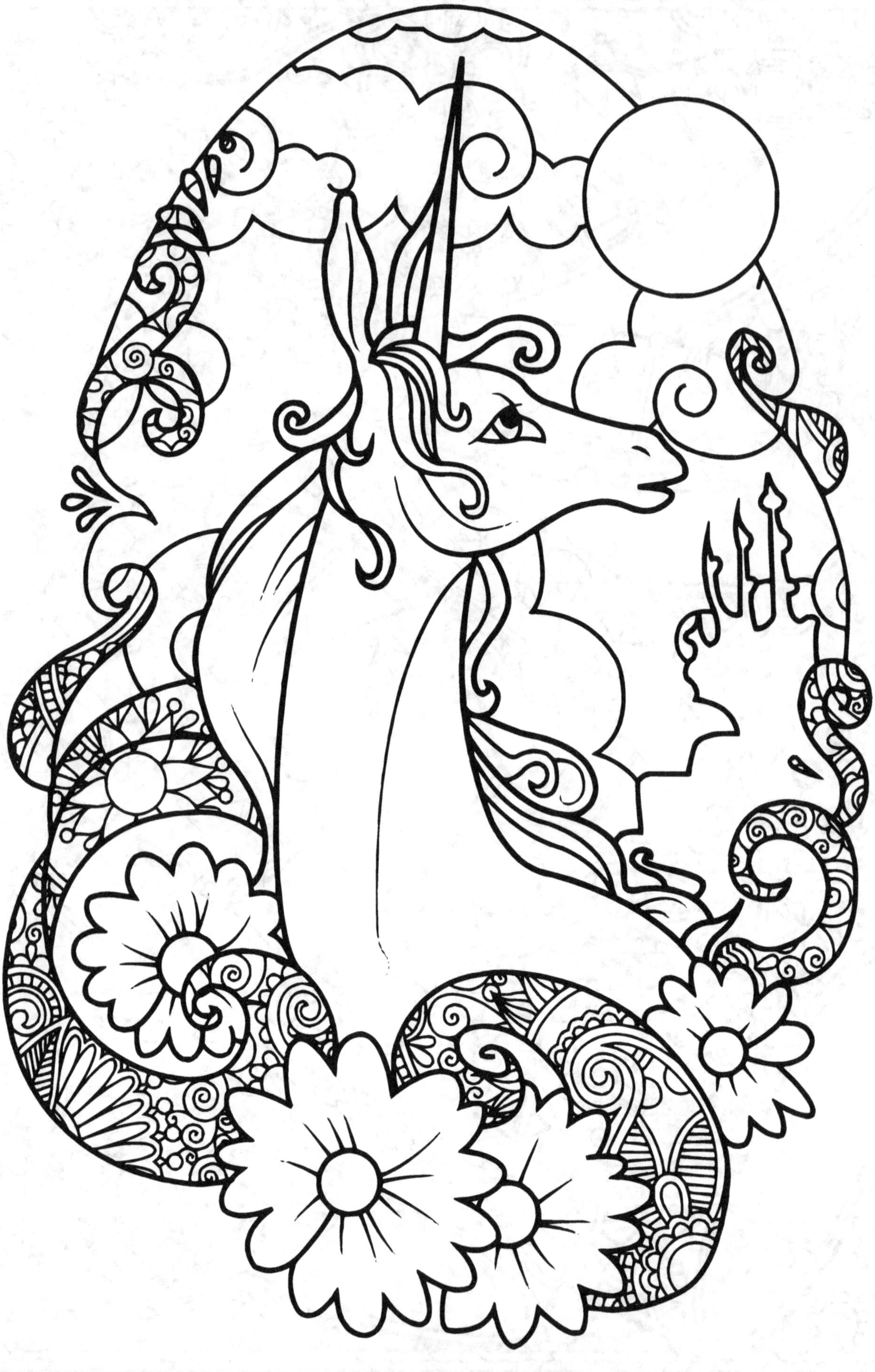

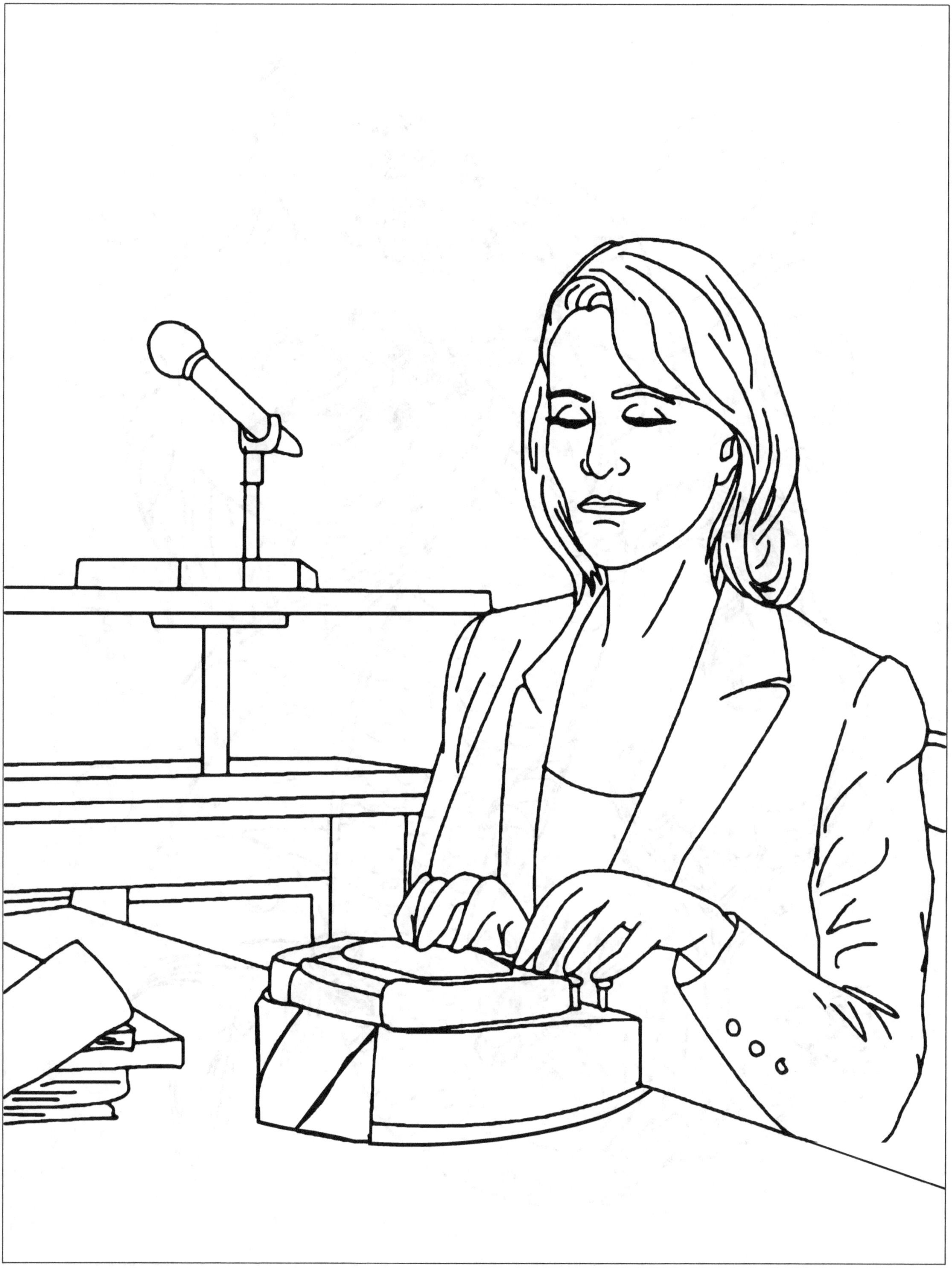

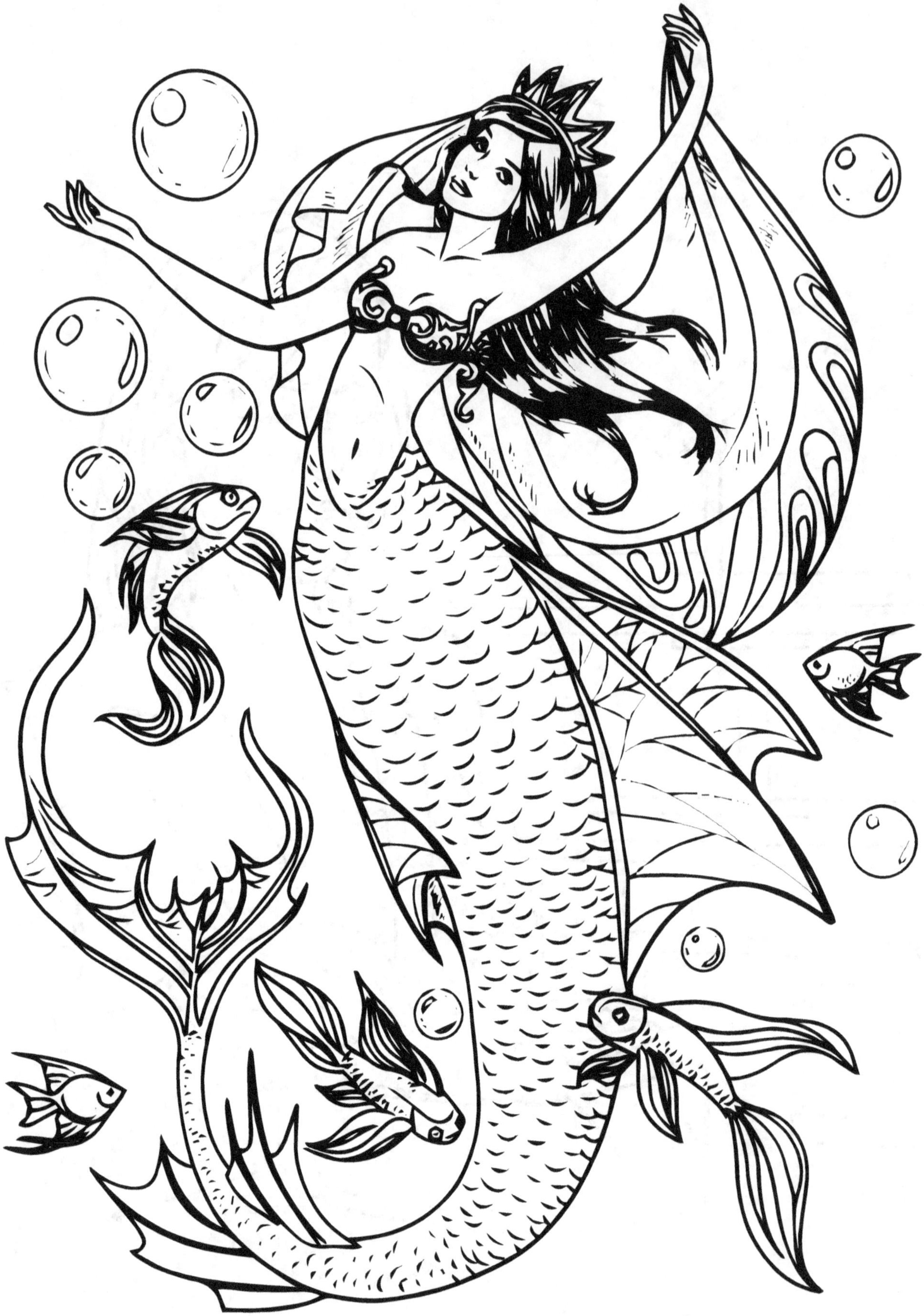

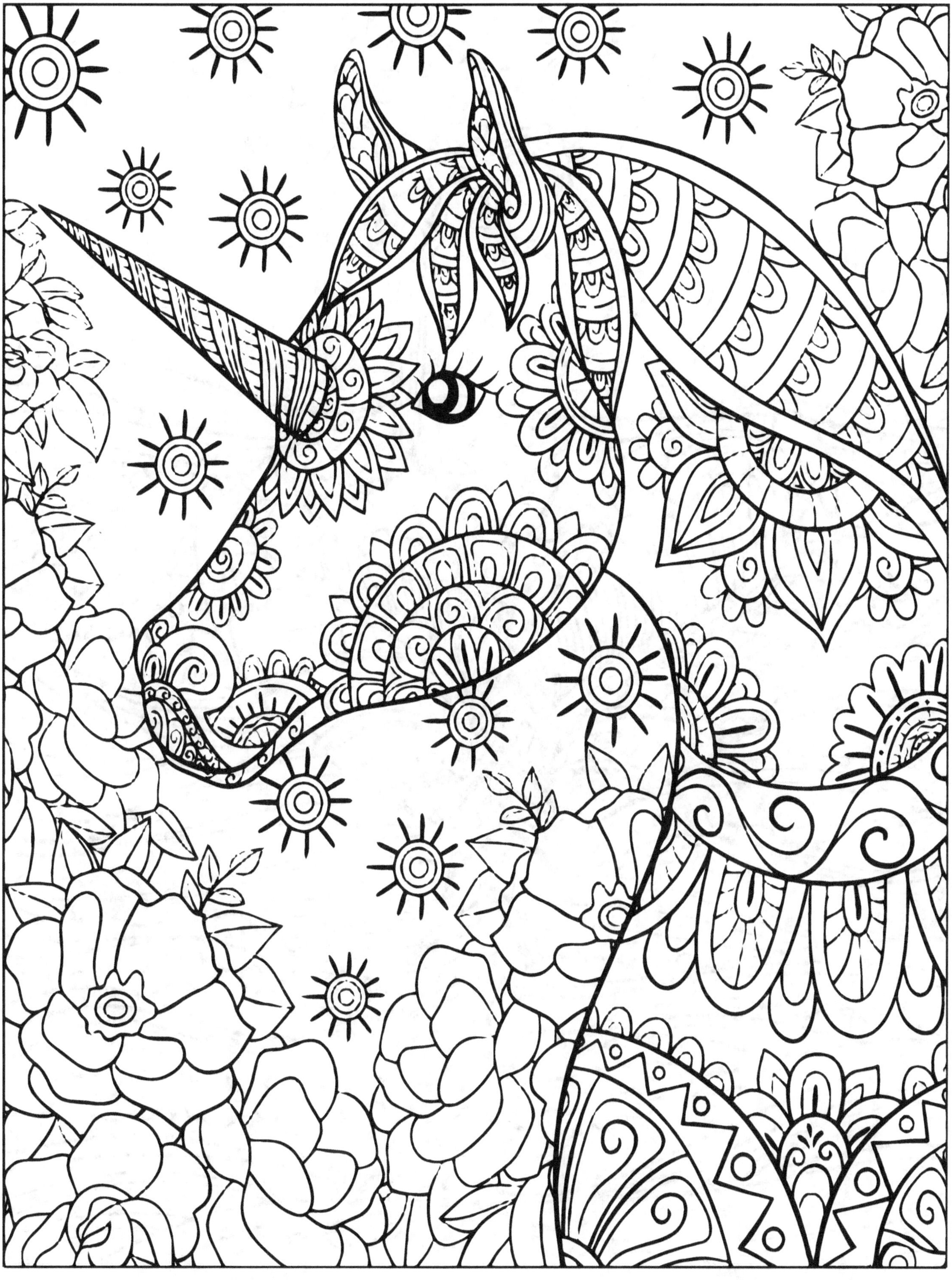

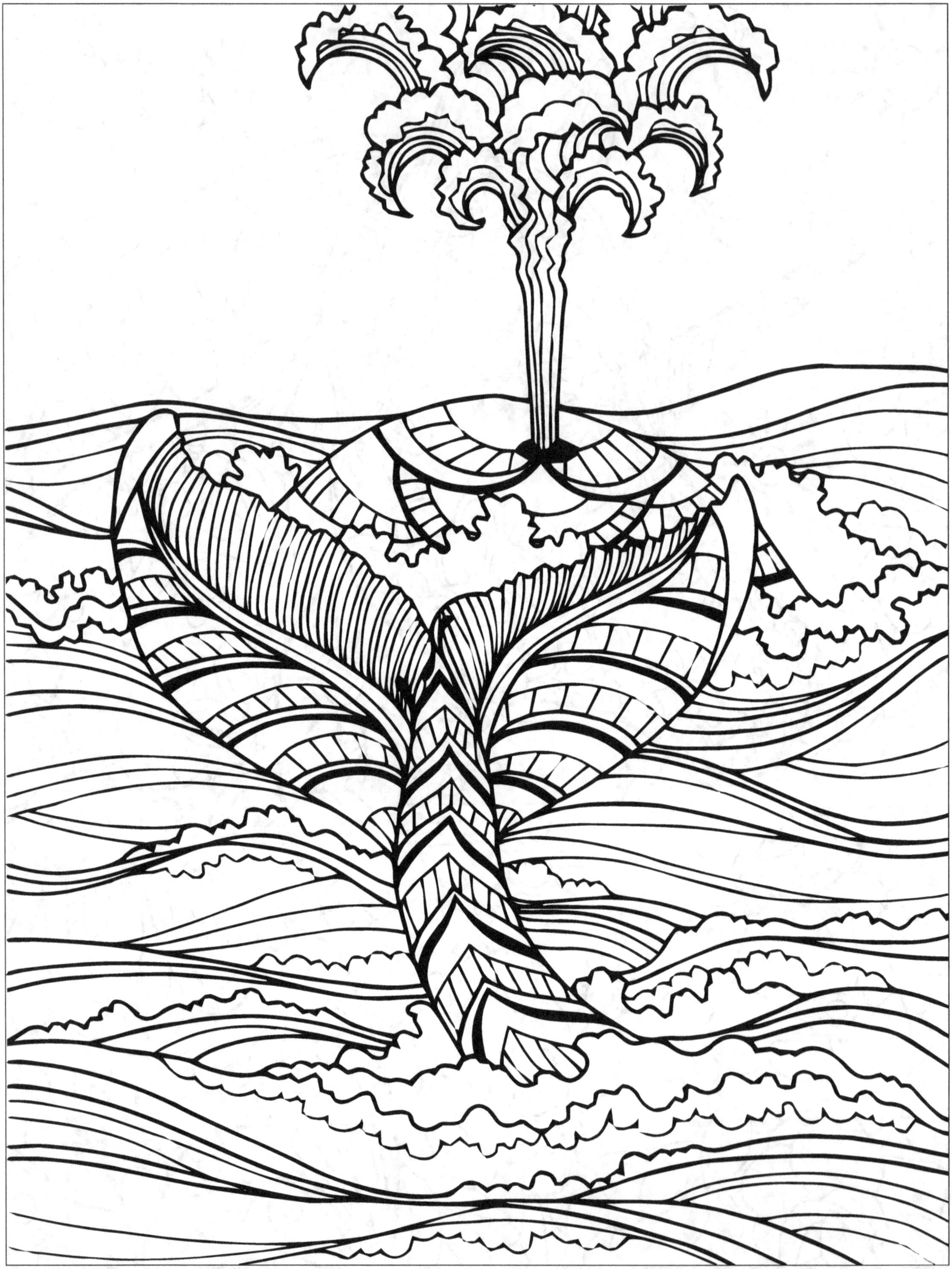

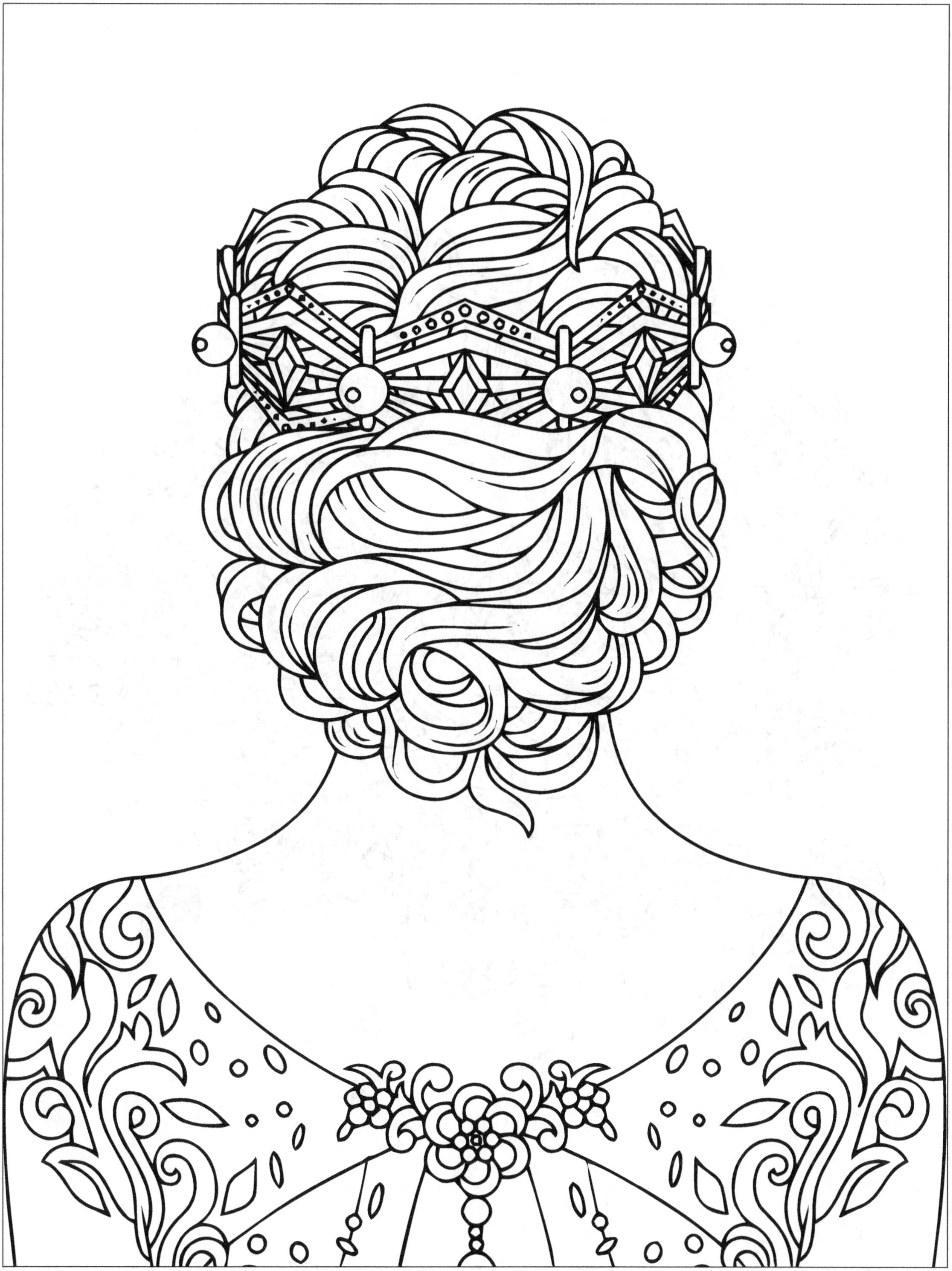

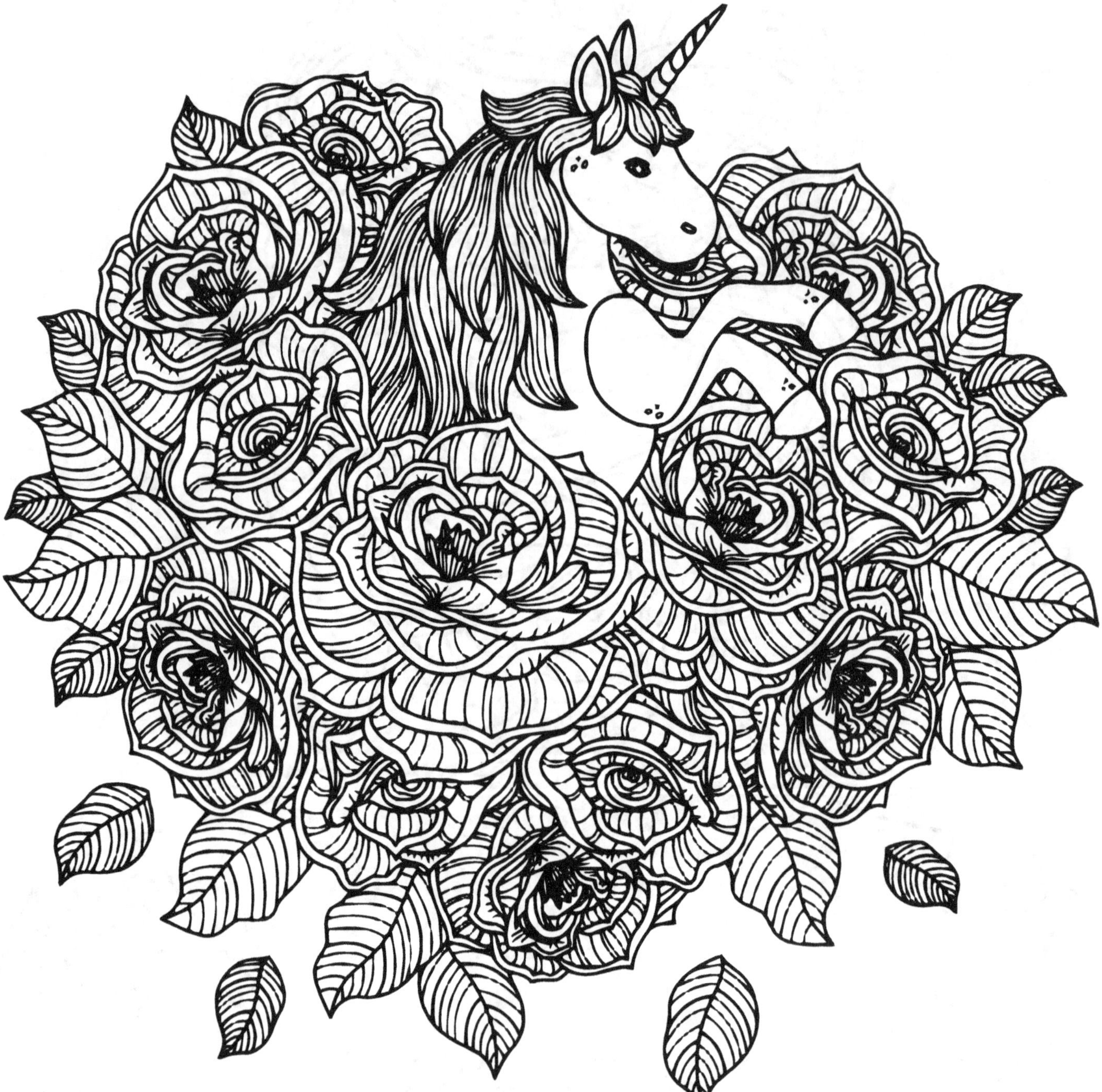

www.ingramcontent.com/pod-product-compliance
Lightning Source LLC
Chambersburg PA
CBHW080817220526
45466CB00011BB/3596
* 9 7 9 8 5 8 9 1 4 8 9 9 2 *